COLLEC

CW00848168

All rights reserved; no part of this book may be reproduced by any means without the publisher's permission.

ISBN: 978-1-913642-46-4

The author has asserted their right to be identified as the author of this Work in accordance with the Copyright, Designs and Patents Act 1988

Book designed by Aaron Kent

Edited by Aaron Kent

Broken Sleep Books (2021), Talgarreg, Wales

Contents

Collected Pamphlets

Aaron Kent

The Rink

2018

Ice Skating, Garden of Eden, 1998

The ice caps were still ideas
rather than liquid forms,
mistakes we promised to
make. You sledded down
Wollaton, while I piled snow
against the door of a man
you never met. I broke my arms
in a race against broken sleep.

I Have Eaten The Moths And Now My Mouth Is Soot

We are three bombs away from night time pressing
halos into the rearview mirror. Why do you shake
when you bleed, when you scream, when we love?
I have cut the ties to my past life, and you are aware
of every mistake I made in transcribing my old notes
onto sheet music.

At first it was the size and shape of the bars, but we
later learnt that every house has a back door, and
every home has an emergency exit. To take away the
pride of an escape is to mute the scenarios in which
we find ourselves at our bravest. I have given myself
the darkest seeds.

I am still uncertain how to proceed with this tumour.
It eats at my soul, and I hear it rapping at the keyboard
when you can't sleep and the hypnotherapy has
deserted me. You are fresh in morning dew, and wearing
the same shapes I gave to that sweet, derelict, old
church we married in.

We never married in.

Teeth As People As Skyscrapers

All I ever wanted was candles on a birthday
cake. One for each year I have written back
to myself and found myself lacking. There is
kindness in the old house yet, but it is not

mine to offer. I am three cups away from an
addiction, home is no longer a place to
down morning crema. Look up, Anthe isn't
mine but I will sketch it onto the

back of every postcard I send. There is room on
all five of my fingers but one, I wish to smother
it in a sign of my stay – I may ride this out or die in
the back room of my grandmother's house.

Moving My Family Into A Den In The Corner Of The House

We are the by-product of every wasted binliner.
It is in these sacks that I want to find you, redemption.
I have built, buildings, built a den, den, den in the back
of my hand read like a fortune teller. We, you and I,
husband and wife, should carry our daughter safely,
so not to bang her skull and make halos the size of
houses. The atom has been split and I am waiting for
it to whisper my name in the sweet embrace of dusk.
It is there we can cower less, coward less, courage
lest the spiders eat our souls. Yours first, then mine,
mine a peach pit, mine a mine, yours the crumb from
a chocolate cake. Our daughter's too fresh to fully
understand the difference between a soul set aside
for the ripening and nuclear devastation.

Counting To Twenty: Self-Portrait 1 / Indecent Exposure

The first person switches the camera
to auto, because we don't know how
to rewind the tape. It is alive outside
again, dear, deer, in headed note paper.
Proper pronunciation requires us to
listen to the camera operator. Eye. Ess.
Oh. Sharpness on a television set. If we
want to document the downfall of
the human race we should, I can, we
should shoulder the blame.

The second person
never lets a split atom
get in the way of a good
photograph.

In Writing: Brother (How's The Family?) Pt. I

The chill has been taken off the front of your throat.
I rest in the palm of your hand like an ant rests
close to the edge and waits to taste the sugar. It is
hard to hear you through the mirror, where the portal
opens and we can finally speak about whether he has
died. I never know, I don't keep your diaries.

It is wasted effort to claw back the minute hand on
your broken pocket watch, all of the weight hangs like
a chipped tooth in a car door. It is not an easy moment,
nor should it be - you have blossomed into the man
I knew you could become, so I have forgotten
how to love you. This is for the best.

In Writing: Brother (How's The Family?) Pt. II

This is for the best placed loser. This is the trophy I'll
put on the mantel when we have guests over. The pasta is
al dente. I'm not sure if you still drink your tea like
that, but just in case I tell the story. Your lips are
dissolvable now just like your politics. Just like our father.
Just like this mirror we have waited in vein to grow wings.

The door is shut on us, he, the grand sum of every halo
Anthe forgot. Take the cannons off the back of our
patches and apply it to the gloss, broken sky, broken sleep.
This is a holiday and a lesson in how to count your dreams
with your eyes open, and where to put the sweet sleep that
calls to you at night. I say pockets.

Amnesty International Workers

[Campaign For Nuclear Disarmament]

The night has calmed to the point we can't process
our features in the dark room. Everything is
no longer a dark room.

You have told our daughter to cover her eyes so
often I worry she will forget how to open them
when the dreams start.

I have wasted our halos on an argument against
the inevitable. Dangerous men become more powerful
with every act.

Every act more powerful with every man.

Every man a temper tantrum away from us.

We remain at the edges, waiting to be excused.

We forget we are working class / We are disposable.

Nothing Changed - Rhetorical Devices

It is that time of year
to leave the den; your sky;
I have kept the memories,
the vale has broken in swansong;
Rue's, opening eyes.

Nothing changes; but for
the questions; how we ask
what we ask, it is in the
tongue; mother's tongue;
we are both forked.

Resolution / CO Monitor

Where the holes in the
ozone layer now press
against our flesh,
we have found a route.

The moths are loose
again, and I have the
remnants of cremation
on the edge of Anthe.

Tertiary colours are
sailors, are the loss of
contact with monocles.
Do not draw landscapes.

It is not mine to harvest.
I am the sum of every
broken wing on every
bird in every nest.

Morning In Retrograde Part III

We have no doorstep for
the mouse, only the sunken
wreck of bougainvillea.

Grant me the serenity
to build a house to build
a home within.

You are near with bandage,
and I, deep in cut, hold the
blood so not to dampen
expectations.

Twenty: Self-Portrait 2 /
Decent Exposure

The last person
takes a snapshot
of the moment and breaks
a glass to celebrate reunion.
In absence of mother.
In absence of absentia.
Absent in Anthe, halos
melt. We are told to show
our daughter
how to spread futility
so fine.

The first person;
you;
enough to stay
in pollution.

The second person;
she;
unfolding faster
than we'd like.

The last person;
I;
not worth the effort
to remain.

Bampy

2018

Budapest, 1956

Vivos Voco

Through good graces and gritted
teeth the crowd sway to the clock's

tick, the grenade's tock. Even
ambulances are ammunition in war.

Esküszünk

Find the skull of your father, read
the novel etched into his stare;

the arms are swollen with loss, the
tongue strained with knots.

Esküszünk, hogy

rabok tovább
Fathers have shrapnel for lungs,
it is how they speak only in

bullets and riddles. Rid the self
of carbon – Imre was a father too.

Nem leszünk!

Father, I've called you three times
        why do you not grace my mirror--

Forradalom

?

He clutches Jimpson Weed
                        hallucinations are welcome in the onyx
curtain
            of nightfall.

She has never seen a live round
                        until Bem Apó is caressed
            friction'd
            with lead. Ice cold – this fragile lilac bullet
            confined to history.

                        He gives her the shrapnel
the fractured metal
                        splintered / dented
            still warm for winter—
                        stained watermelon red
                                    flesh.

        "I give you my love
                        everything I have to offer
                in my country"

                        The desertion is imminent
            waiting at the fringes
                        of conversation
as an unfed tiger
                        sipping poison in Ueno Zoo.

"Hol sírjaink domborulnak,
unokáink leborulnak"

The two-forint coin is early
in cotton soft sheets lain beside Hösök Tére
and the blossom of sirens
carrying the living – live rounds – round to

"Throw yours in the Danube
leave us to rest infinity"

He would not be wrapped
in barbs or nettle

lest it tears his flesh
and drag him back

to the tulip'd Danube.

Mortuos Plango

Daughter, I have sent you two ropes:
             one to hang yourself with
the other for the neighbours to ring

             each successive year in.
15 new years. Every mute swan
             sings the Nemzeti Dal in

rhythm with genocide, and I hear
             you calling the Soviets back
to stand hand-in-hand. I am not

             disappointed – for I too
call the living, yet I spill blood
             into my father's boots for

freedom and the pastures of Hungary.
             Dead- I will still weep sweet
particles of lachrymator. Drag me

             and tie me in barbed wire
there is a corner reserved for us,
             unless you keep your rope

and swear to press free passage
             into your fresh scars.

Felkelés

I mourn the dead
        as the slaves of the Austrian empire
                in tyre-black boots dust stampedes

Forgotten the native tongue
        Magyar as the gold coin silver too
                left to enchant Államvédelmi Hatóság

Berszik Baden the colour of dusk
        deep rouge nightmares of refuge
                refugee status in deep claret lipstick

We vow (esküszünk)
        we vow (esküszünk)
                that we will be slaves no longer

The old refrains pressing
        against your father's portrait
                in the back corner of the attic

He wears a beard
        heavy with the weight of wire wool
                confined to will of lightening bolts

Calamity sweats the blues
        of bathing in the Danube river
                wearing a wedding ring too loose

Leave it for my blood
        signed and certified as blood
                to weep carat on ocean waves

I call the living
        I mourn the dead
                I pray to the red cross

Fragile bullets of lilac
        fragility expressed as a flower
                the calm face rotting in motion

Steel my resolve and sing
        your father's name when
                they ask you it in school

In dearest Romania
        the neighbour with noose
                the lowest knot on the monkey's fist

        All the shepherd's nights
                ring in the dawn translucent
                        against the backdrop of

                camomile as resurrection
                        of the body's natural
                                impulse to flee.

Fulgura Frango

Borders are drawn gold
in permanence in media

res cherry blossom
falls over at Margitsziget

and from Artúr's
longest stretch of aquamarine

every monk and nun
flocking like gallow'd

swans to the scene can
only pray in some other

mother's tongue can only
dream of Zenél☒ szök☒kút

saccharine waters arch
to drums stampede glass

shatter hell cry fury
wait –

Here, Röszke, breaks the barbs
and cradles the heart

in transport to adoptive
presence. Every monk,

and every nun, drawn
and quartered by morning's

first hymn. Place hands where
the body is immune,

and give seasonal ailments-
the best excuse to leave

is to confess a sore throat
and hide the tear in

fabric where skin once
met. Now flooded—

the Danube run crimson
in this barbed wire night.

Hösök Tére

The National Song stamped

      across my forearms

and etched into the leaves

on every tree we

pass over dry land

      on the climb

to the second coming

of the Mayflower

      in turbulence it is

that I call the living,

I mourn the dead---

Budapest, 2000

--I break your heart.

Dear Artúr,

It was good to hear from you, I also sing in my sleep and wait for cuckoos to march. I am sorry I cannot come home just yet, I was hoping to be with you for your birthday but I will have to miss it this year. How does the sky look in Redruth? Is it still screaming? I have begun drowning myself a little bit every night so that when the flood comes I will be immune.

I searched for the two-forint but only found half. I'd like you to imagine what the Danube looks like so many years after the fact – it is less than it was, it is less than it was. I have written to you twice and you can show your father one. He is not worth a nickname.

Please, send my love to the mines.

Your best friend,

Bampy

Redruth, 1996

Stannum

This history
is not yours
            to keep in your pocket

you wear
your scars in bullets
            in your native tongue

South Crofty
will not collapse
            angles in contradiction

your front room
broken shades
            later I will wait for the bus

as a man
now residing
            in your bedroom

beats a doll
all fists and anger
            to intimidate the school kids

I saw my father
amid your warnings
            and watched red blood cells

stampede to his feet
against the wall
            against the spray of curry

he couldn't cook
like you
                    couldn't season the burning

           hand against heat
radiator bumps
                    and a fall from height like yours

           maybe that's the aim
feel your historical
                    hate in stories I've heard

           the statue
a lady of the night
                    as my mother called it

           and the story
of your father
                    my mother's father's father

           returning from payment
to hold your neck
                    and swing us both from the ceiling.

Domhwelans

'Si deve suonare tutto questo pezzo delicatissimamente
e senza sordino'

It was winter

                                        [blue]

when they split the bark
          and married it
with chemicals.

          I was bound.

          Molten salts.

          Press Johannes Gutenberg's words
                    onto the population--
                    --every byproduct of some father's racism.

There are 290 boxes to think outside of,
to play both   summer
                                        and winter

                                        [red & blue]

for 14 times,
          14 midnights,
                    14 full moons.

Some impromptu fantasy/I still call my father's name in my sleep,
          in triple p dynamic,
                    so I don't disturb the neighbours
          and give them reason to care.
          I like the nonchalance.

          I like calling the cat in
                    without thinking the neighbours
                    might try to lend a hand.

I hallucinate, spring

                    [yellow]
                    out of bed when grass is luminescent
in twilight.   Pavor Nocturnus.

Killing either God,

                              or my father
                    twenty years too late for it to make a
                    difference.

                    Buy me delta sleep,
rip the turpentine and soap
                    from my glands.
Give me beautiful sleep architecture,

                    house my dreams in autumn
                    [brown]

Cuprum

I sing your
anthem in
my sleep
and count
dandelions
in postured
glory among
the ways we
could both
better our
selves if given
the temerity
to call hösök
tére and the
sirens now
expanding into
white noise

sleep in this
hoover'd bliss
and press sugar
paper as duvets
you still wear
the weight of
our adventure

Omsay

Your daughter is a timebomb

        Bampy

                her wires are crossed

    again and

        again.

She cannot hear how

                your son-in-law runs his

        nails down a chalkboard

    but the tonal majors

            have come back

        Bampy

        you'd like this song.

Your daughter has two regrets:

            and neither are correct

    she should regret

cleaning the blood from the bath

            with that sour stench

bleach

        because his blood does not pool

    will not Pool.

    When I see my father in rigor mortis

        Bampy

            I imagine him swallowing

    the oceans of women

he loved enough

    to never tell them

he loved them.

Hevva Hevva

We both mourn the dead
      in rhythmic prayer
for tin mines. Your home
      built upon an
ancient burial ground
      before you gave it
to ancient rituals. Remember
      when you got that
German Shepherd and she
      ran away – that is
when I realised permanence

            is not housebound.
      The tunnels beneath us crawl
            with every wasted meal
      besmirched by a toddler's
            face. All I ever wanted
      were candles on a birthday cake.

We both mourn the living
      and play the river
for every kintsugi soul
      repaired with
VHS. You can bring the ends
      together but you
can't make them meet.
      I don't think you
ever wanted me either, but
      at least you were
happy enough to borrow me—

Fore Street

--and happy
enough to give me back / I found another

family / lived Venezuela post-Hungary /
they gave me a ghost / still watches me

shower / your house has aged / the wall
pock-marked with pebbles / the garden

mostly alcohol
soiled / it was like this before / your stare

built I into every room / the weight of
the clouds / cannonballs for hail storms /

you as a giant / watched me sleep for fear
I would see the cracks / I see them now /

--I break
/ I break the thunderbolts /

Sheffield, 2006-2016

You are warm
in mirror
and recluse
in frame.

Reprint.

You ARE WARM
IN mirror
and recluse in sgram
frame.

Repriunt

Tou are wqMR
IN TRMIRROR
SAND arenckude
in framre
#
reoruint
t
tou sre warm
in muirror
and rcluse ri
in fdrmae

trorunt
gtiy
tiu are warm
in m,irror
and telcise
in reame

reprint

you are warm
in mirror
and recluse
in drame.

Tertiary Colours

2018

I.

When I wake I am bound to it, crying out
for rapid eye movement, for beautiful sleep
architecture. I am wed to my dreams and
watching Operation Antler from the other side
of the Danube – where our cats present mice
as if the world just needs a little blood, and a
bow. I sit absent at the breakfast table and
spill my secrets to the toast, the jam, the
darling black coffee. I reel off problems to
present to the pandas in the broken men's
club, chilled windows and broken radiators
breathe winter into my hooves. My head
prepares to split and welcome a new spring.

The horn comes
before the eye.

II.

I pull slowly away from inability under the madness of infinity, and wear the charms under the weight of midday. With warmth comes effort, comes glory, comes a supreme, release from an effective frame of reference (Kent, A., 1989. *Post-Traumatic: A Study of Engaging with the Joy of Terror.* Redruth: St Day Road). Tertiary colours exist for the covers of discontinued poetry books, and the moods of forgotten sailors. There are warnings in the shape of broken branches and migraines.

Tissue
replaces cartilage
III.

The editor suggests brown bread works better / and a poached egg is marginally more romantic than a fried egg – some metaphor about the glory / of reproduction / I'm ignorant / clawing / the sharpened edges of my sister's retreat / into the neighbouring crooked hill / I find solace / in pen marks / little notes / and a dictionary / with no pages / I have superglue for fingers / and wear my clothes with all the grace of a dying man / phone lines are designed to catch people / who lean out of train windows.

The bone is infected
by osteoclasts.

I am Perseus in somnambulance [again] / caught in daydreams / of auxiliary machinery spaces where a career touch / burns hydraulic and bleeds ballast / we broke cardinal rules / fell victim to cardinals / the ceiling is glass in tertiary / colours / stained with my mentor's nuclear fluid / radiation / is a plague of numbers / 51°22'47.1"N 30°06'50.6"E / a protective measure / a hand straying / through the exclusion zone / a muffled scream / I lean out of the window / and feel summer brush the top of the glass.

IV.

I crawl disfigured into kintsugi, hear the pikatrapp chimes call me for Geppetto. There is little fight left, and trace amounts of salt.

I am unbound, treading water in military
overalls disguising

a three-piece suit. The charms
wear tired eyes a sign they have ingest-
ed too much today, all two hundred
meters of water drawn from a flood in
Tolgus to a death in an Atlantic prison.

I will not sleep in
blue skies when there are
genes to wear as a raincoat.
My skull reforms, I am no
longer wrapped in gold. The
psychic

w   h   o
warned me of an-
gels the size of
houses has clear-
ly never sat in a
library and read
the old dreams of
unicorn skulls.

Something else for the dog
to chew on.

VI.

Broken hands and broken mouths. Regret and
resentment and hand-washed clothes.

From the French
meaning before
the eye. Antoillier.

V.

I   sit   as   a   representation   of   Piaget's   refus-
al   to   repeat   generations,   watching   solar   powered
windmills   direct   traffic   across   the
sjóndeildarhnífuringur.   Methods   to   reject
introspection include:
pretending to know how to meditate,
glorifying failures,
burning through the night.
I close my eyes and let the reservoir fill with sharks and
hate, remnants of a tin mine past – that dance of crim-
son on my inner canthal has betrayed me, led me back
down the grey tiled garden. I'm striking bark at midnight,
striking   the   rats   from   the   torpedoes,
sutoraiku   two   inches   from   nuclear
destruction. There are two cinemas showing *The Sopranos*, nei-
ther lets me in, I'm left to drink wine from the tap.

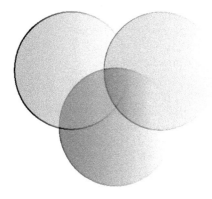

VII.

With fear and glory in equal measure.

VIII.

There's a vague sense of my mother / carrying me above snakes / my head bowed to the sound of an operator / begging for another chance to revive the child / a hint of my brother / breaking my heart / a daughter who grew up too fast – became a robot.

Became a feature of the room, some jewelled ornament. I'm never in the same room when I wake / sometimes there are sixty seven seats / other times I'm ironing / in the kitchen rubbing soap on the inside of my seams / they won't catch me biting through pistachio shells / spitting sunflowers / into our cemeteries – there's a tree nobody can touch / it's too famous.

A tree for an ambient airport.

My back aches from carrying the charms / through needles and nettles / there was a pickaxe / in the cabin / a spray of blood and ninety degrees / of indecision / we hid in the background / and found heaven at the bottom of a manhole / I choked her for protection / forced my arm into the bars / at the top of the bed / there were malicious men, damaged crooks, broken thieves / who wanted glory / I poured myself into her / forced their knives / into my back / kept the embryo golden.

I am not meant to carry gold / just to throw it on the beauty. I lost sight of the doorway and clung to the sheets / a state of construction / as my mind wept daylight across my retina / the editor remembers / where the walls were, but moves them three inches / inwards – claustrophobia is an interesting trait / the editor / wants me to choose a Windsor knot / relate it to my daddy issues / maybe a story about a job interview.

"Your dad never taught you to shave / tie a tie / ride a bike" ...yes / unprepared / and covered / in the stench of his ink.

IX.

I saw myself in Rough Park,
        floating
                unaided
                        using the same lines over and over.

I never meant to be repetitive,
        to lock myself away
                with the broken records
                        scratched firmly against pikatrapp.

X.

The cat knows what I'm trying to say, the rhyme scheme I've given up on, and the words I can't mouth [even in my healthiest friendship circle]. I no longer hear foxes at night and I worry it's because they thought I was a voyeur. I watched them tear apart the bins in the hope of finding my name and address, stealing my identity, then having to deal with all my repressed torment. Theories of glasses being half full or empty ignore the fact that somebody has to pour the liquid in, and I forget to drink some days. Most days. Forget to breathe some times. Most times. Forget to tell new people that I was touched by some dude in some way. A wholly inappropriate way. I'd like to see the foxes deal with that.

Nutritional dependency
has caused me to fall apart
again.

XI.

Demons sit in the dentist's waiting room,
picking the sand from their teeth and I watch
my addiction to black coffee form a perfect
black sphere in the centre of my iris. I wake
sober in the city centre and plan an ancient
God's murder by forgiving every Krossdeath.

I am discarded
as calcium and phosphorus.

I begin a new obsession with tape recorders, so
I can play my thoughts back every Thursday to
the kintsugi club. 'Note to self: His hand was
clammy. Note to self: You can still smell the
grease on his neck at night. Note to self: He
followed you back on that flight from Glasgow
to Cornwall.'

I am hunted: Beam, palm, brow, bez
or bay, trez or tray, royal, and surroyal.

I serve an arabica – robusta blend to the family
with the toothpaste smiles, and wonder what
would happen if they introduced me to their
hero. A man with a kind nature, a good heart,
and the stench of my shame still ironed into
his epaulets.

XII.

Even in winter the sky still glows for a man with too many suns to notice the disappearance of a single star.

XIV.

When I climb stairs I jigsaw star.

pikatrapp pikatrapp. pikatrapp pikatrapp pikatrapp pikatrapp. When I climb stairs I remain silent.

XV.

When I leave the broken club [the kintsugi starts to form] and the stories begin to dissipate, I am reminded of how little testosterone I have left after he tore it from my system. I walk through the watchmaker's alley, and rekindle my sorry excuses. I could never kill my God, could never leave the stairs, could never break his hydraulic hand before he became hydraulic. AMS II/III is still deep in my flesh, still whispering shrapnel in my ear and cleaning wounds in his bunk. I keep my hands soft, don't let dirt cling to them [won't piss with dirty fingers because it may feel like his grip again, the coarseness of his flesh, the dexterity of his digits]. Is this what a novel is supposed to look like? I consider changing the scope of the story, make it less biographical, a pseudo-biopic with a happy ending. Instead of tearing out my soul, we could've sat down with a cup of coffee – brewed a mug of arabica and opened up. He'd tell me he wanted to violate me, smash my back, and squeeze my throat. We could discuss what this really means for him, the ways in which he could better himself [*next time make a list of the ways you want to scar me for life, but read it aloud once to yourself and throw it away after*]. He could have two sugars, I could have none, he could make the joke that I'm sweet enough, and I'd live safe in the knowledge that it was just a joke, not an invitation to unzip my flies and rain nuclear waste down upon me. But writing is sometimes honest, sometimes true, sometimes a reason for an exorcism. So I keep in the finer points, ignore the trivial need for fictionalisation, and burn the fragments that encourage mediocrity.

I was reclaimed
to build him a gun,
to build him a dagger.

XVI.

When I watch the charms find glory in the
dead of night, I capture every mark on her
face. I make imprints of our potential and
determine that with enough luck maybe I
won't burden our child with much of my DNA
at all.

XVII.

My favourite part was when I kicked the walls
until I bled because I swore I saw a door there.
I have seen men with knives carve my
name into deaths they had sewn in the wallpaper.

I watched my brother choke from the
weight of the roof, sans hurricane, sans life.
There are always spiders, always
tarantulas, always the size of small cars.

Sometimes snakes remind me I
pissed the bed until I was twelve.
When the room caves in I leap
to the defence of the dead.

My hobbies involve watching
as strangers' eyes bleed.
I've become an expert
at breaking my knuckles

but you've become
spectacular at holding me
until I stop crying,
and lulling me back

to sleep.

XVIII.

I am informed there aren't enough colours, not enough title-nodding references, or little nudges between the reader and the ideas presented. The editor wants something a little more oblique, a little less opaque. Let the reader watch you / dissolve.

He wore his pride aloft as horns.

XIX.

I had never been primary / enough to paint the sky / in broad strokes / just a tertiary colour burnt from the brush / of a broken hand / the mood of forgotten sailors / mermaids as medusa (Hayter, C., 1826. *A New Practical Treatise on the Three Primitive Colours Assumed as a Perfect System of Rudimentary Information.* London).

XX.

With fear and glory embalmed in a house in Redruth.

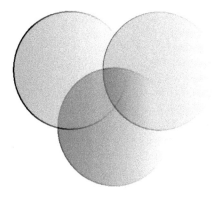

XXI.

You are not the sum of your parts, or the collection of news stories some western media thinks will sell front pages to bored conspiracy theorists. You were, and still are, a kid torn from Bangladesh and promised a brighter start in southwest England. You were a couple of years older, but put in our class, and you were quick to gain friends. You gave us free meals at your restaurant, and we gave you immunity from the idiocy of children taught by parasites to hate. You wore the same backpack every day, and you never quite learnt to look both ways before crossing the road. You were welcomed and loved. You were an important part of my childhood. You were mocked by my mother – who looked both ways and crossed the road when she saw you with that backpack, or joked that you should leave it outside the house for fear that it contained a bomb. My mum, the white, suburban, bored conspiracy theorist who swore she believed in God.

There is no genetic correlation.

XXII.

I still write lyrics for a friend,
and every time I struggle to
write pop in a way that warrants
mainstream interest. I want to
write of torture, and car
batteries, and shots of whiskey,
and the glory of fatherly
stubble, and broken arms, and
broken wings, and torn feathers,
and blisters, and triangular
junctions, and pika, and trapp,
and the fate of a defeatist
childhood, and living room
truces, and renegade brothers,
and frozen ground, and marked
men, and forced dancing, and
drug-addled weightlifting, and
speed in cakes, and Hell's
Angels, and shanking people in
Acton, and a Hungarian man
trying to make a difference, and
noses pushed to ceilings, and
backs slapping floors, and
hands pressed tight to radiators,
and Princess Diana taking over
all the TV channels, and
Muhammad's backpack, and tin
Skodas, and Hey Arnold as a
genuine depiction of family,
and the blues, and the Blues,
and the holly bush, and the
drunk neighbours, and the
stoned neighbours, and the
stabbed neighbours, and
scooter rallies, and grill pans,
and the memory of sex toys,
and ironing at five am, and
sleeping at three am, and

waking at four am, and falling down stairs still asleep, and breaking toes, and breaking a finger, and breaking my heart, and the dogs who were never walked, and auxiliary machine space number two on the third level, and some chief, and the mind's ability to block things out, and Grandad on breathing equipment, and locked in a caravan by the beach, and bedroom floors at Christmas, and the babysitter, and the old friend, and my sister's mum, and my sister, and those eighteen lost years, and the inability to cry, and the pillow of my face, and bipolar with no support, and I think it's probably time I stop writing about this shit but I can't

but I can't

but I can't

and I still blame you in every way, in every moment I have free I blame you for the mess I have made of things.

XXIII.

...and it was there you presented / didn't wait for a response / your strength on display / your fertility ready to squeeze / tight / your overgrown antlers / my underwhelming tertiary colours / we fought / I lost / you took your prize amongst the blood / and / diesel / I can't remember if I swelled from the bruises / or stayed limp from fear / but for a moment I turned red / I was primary / I became singular / and all it needed was a lack of consent / and a cut that wouldn't stop bleeding.

My velvet – lost

My bones – dead

My experience – the footnote of a short trip across the Atlantic.

XXIV.

When I wake / I am still bound to it, begging for sleep architecture from a fashion magazine. I am the moods of forgotten sailors, picking the superglue from broken fingers, broken toes. Mount Amara bound, your radiation was a curse, and the charms brought summer to translucent windows – more can be ingested today, but never pikatrapp. I wrapped the bed in gold but still found djöfaðirullin on the sjóndeildarhnífuringur where angels the size of car tires carried me over snakes. [still hating the fifth and sixth, still mad at cheap tricks]. [am happier with the fifth, now love the sixth]. With glory and a robot daughter leaving ambient airports for a shot at freedom. Floating unaided, always locked away. I forget to fill my lungs while the foxes have left from the boredom of begging me to breathe again. Krossdeath has never been the excuse I needed it to be, it never boarded a flight to my witness protection, it never wore my shame like a medal I couldn't receive. Even in winter I repeat myself. I'm rebuilding for the future, splicing my genes with the *charms* and a bright vessel to fill with hope. To put candles in their birthday cake. I watched my brother choke my presence from his life and still didn't call enough attention to the colour palette of famous artists. The bruises still leak into my skin, and you still caress me in my most anxious hours. When I climb stairs I am reminded of cameras, and oak and a promise not to tell anyone because they'd be angry, and you'd be in a lot of trouble.

Without antlers
I'll grow tusks.

Djöfaðirullin Parade

There is a fire
in the corner
of
the care
home,
and I will never
douse it
or let you light
cigarettes
on the edge of the ash
or flames.

It exists
purely
as a tutorial,
a light on the sjóndeildarhuringur
to show you
how to join
the djöfaðirullin parade
when your wnigs
are nothing but
the cancerous
stumps
of a forgotten goat herder.

Love me in ways
that the Beach Boys
can never
sing
about
because
the hallucinogenics
aren't strong enough
to warp
camera flashes
into signs of better
men.

There is no reason
to find sanity
in the corner
of
a broken bathtub.

You are the weakness
I cradle at night
and the rapidfire
in my lungs,
you are every
locked door
on a hospital ward,
and you are more
than just
a mistake
Guð pressed
into the book
that holds
my hourglass.

St Day Road

2018

The Entrance

our neighbour filled his lungs
with regret in a damp garage
under an early morning's halogen moon.
his kids still went to school,
cars still hugged at high speed,
birds still sung of flights and funerals.
i kept each tragedy like a loving parent
making notches to catalogue their children's height.

born screaming from the headlight glass embedded in my back
i tried breaking my arms to grow wings
and kept each splinter from our terraced house
in hungary.
- my ghost missed my birth
was too busy nailing a 10 to the door
so i knew which age to kill my heroes -
even in winter the sky is full of suns.

Hallway

i lived in full view of your mirror
as i sat spinning gold coins, silver too,
on the mosaic path to the oak farm.
crutches lay by the door, a reminder

of the kintsugi in your knee.
drown me in the river or burn me in the cave,
no matter how you split my pieces ill never
form nests in the shadow of your youth.

Living Room

you saw a ghost
spin coins in our
mirror, taught it
that heroes are demons
are dead. a shattered
knee isnt an excuse
to kill the number
15.

you joked about
how to clean
a car post suicide.
how to keep
value and wash
the piss stains out.
use bleach.
ventilate.

you applauded a man,
as a family watching tv,
who tread a fine line
between shitting
himself and making
a fart joke.
i watched
hey arnold and cried
at the state of my genes.

sometimes a standing ovation is just an excuse to leave.

Kitchen

i scouted exits
dancing under our broken ceiling
as cuckoos sung.
my wings never grew
but i forced a feather
to scrawl 'kill your demons'
in our dead skin cells.
it grew for six years.
you built a blue eyed boy
from the ash
of my shit toned irides
and lived to watch
me become
your greatest mistake.
even in the darkest days
your sky was full of suns.

Stairs

the bombs
the flash
oask burnt
pikatrapp

Bedroom

i found medusa in the dungeon
and was carried to l'inferno
where ancestral voices
cried 'hui aware'
i was perseus!
somnambulist!
mount amara bound!
alone to watch my blood as heires.

Back Bathroom

bleach pooled on frozen tiles
where blood mixed ash
with smoke. after the torture
ghosts placed me on my bike,
they were the wrong ones
to haunt me, or wash my mistakes.
i paid my demons in gold coins, silver too,
to teach me to write my blood.

Loft

was it our revenant who smashed our roof
crushing my cot, exposing our core
and ending the sickness
or me, in dream, stealing history?

i retell the hurricane
as if i lived it rather than you
reading XLIII, me unborn,
bats and owlets builders in the roof.

these ancient winds will never be mine
though ill cherish them as you dont,
like i keep my demons fed, inside,
beside a voice that weeps.

i still bleed your storm
onto dead paper, mute.
fifteen, ten, fourty three, lost.
with no roof, an empty sky has no sons.

Upstairs

someone saw you in the bathroom
    floating
        unaided
            held together by string.
I never saw those weaknesses
    locked myself away
        with the giants
            pressed tight to our windows.

Exit

there were doctors at the gates
exposing my lungs
to bloodied, bruised, latex faces.
i forced my skull
against the vanity mirror
so violence could be a lesson to learn.
we filled the reservoir
with sharks and hate
and remnants of our tin mine past.
the bombs kept falling
with bleach and ash and exits and ex
itsandexitandexitandexitandexitandexitandexitandexitandexit

The Last Hundred

2019

Boscaswell, Via Holy Well

...perhaps to house the widows
of soot-smoked bodies, or to
carry the canary home from
two hundred fathoms of fishermen,
miners too. This granite village
gathers variety along the coast -
hornfels and killas. Boscaswell
washes in the scent of lime, helps the
locals survive the storm - through
no funding, no funnelling down to
the working class. Geevor's
veins run black through the downs
and pull cassiterite through conflict,
only the ants can watch the ocean
spray the shape of a Pinder table. Visit
the well and pray to the Boxer,
sing for Bridgework, worship
Lawry in the glory of a history
oft repeated never to be relived.
This is not Santa Cristina or St
Mary of the Spring or the
Chalice Well. There are no
pilgrimages to decay, nor
remnants of a makeshift chapel
or cairn. The village split the
river, cured the irides of
fishermen, miners too, left
leeches plump with the blood
of buccas...

Cairn Field, Geevor

Cairn to mark the spot the tin mines fell,
the day the miners turned in their tools,
evaporation of the red ford from the source.

Crust carried from the depths
to replace the crumbs taken from the
sole of every photographer's shoes.

A rock pile built by infants, carried by juniors, demolished by adolescence.
All these schools moulded in the shape of another language, given culture
as a white stripe on a black cross, begged to stop teaching the language.

In descending order of importance across
the coastline of West Penwith all the tin
and fish have been replaced by abstract graves.

Reserves of worthless economy,
currency burnt by angry knockers.
A flood of lethargy - the eighth plague.

Economy has to pivot on a whim here. Cairns held aloft
by the bruised hands of holidaymakers, a sign to the county
that they heard the cry for help, and gave all they could in footprints.

There are few safeguards and no pullies
or levers among the uneven structures.
Perhaps designed for a landslide -

perhaps patented for a fall.

Madron Well

Bathe in the spring of the lake
and return to your younger self,
golden and sunburnt on the hill.
Through blackthorn and hawthorn
there are broken sticks to fasten
and drop into the well's bucket.
Cavitation is a symbol of wedlock.
If the demons of infirmary

come burning and headstrong,
point to the clouties in the
hedgerows and ask for peace.
Beltane is for fertility
and a triangle of nudity.
Walk three times clockwise
and rest on St Madern's Bed.
Be ready to take your turn

to walk through the devil's door.

Near Madron

'Would you come brighten my corner?
A lit torch to the woodpile' - Frightened Rabbit

Here lyeth bodyes of wood,
catapults, and a call to arms
        for ten children
under the breast of stained glass
[west window].

        Enter two feet wide,
        two feet thick, two
feet into the well through thickets
        of perennial nettle tea
        [Urtica Dioica].

Dig under the wooden cromlêh
and find bone, half a skull,
        and twenty reasons
to leave for the crickstone.
[RIALoBRAN CUNoVAL-fIL-].

        Alas no gold or luck
        for the falling rocks.
A thunderstorm for three centuries
        atop Mulfra Hill.
        [Mulfra Quoit].

 Two dolls' heads lie trunkless
in the ruth, red, watched from
        high abandon, eyes
set in a perfect hill castle.
[Ch'ûn Castle. Chy-an-oon].

        Another landscape
        annexed, torn apart
and rekindled for fire wood
        in the homes of dukes.
        [ILFORD 100 DELTA PRO].

Near Sancreed

Marked as the decimal point in the last hundred, the birds flock as the remaining digits, rounded up to a murder of one. Set under Credan's sky, this chei - now chei golyow - holds bark to its chest and lets rigid claws awaken the night with frosted windows. Yet, more home than krow, overgrown and underfoot, the last county gives back to nature, and lets glory give grace to crowded places. Above the loam there are stories of patricide and punishment, the only land to not touch the sea or welcome the tears of mermaids.

Near Trencrom Hill

Trecobben cannot hide
       from Cormoran
              behind these
                    onopordum acanthium.

Swinging a hammer
       from Trencrom
              to the skull
                    of Cormelian.

Incur the wrath
       from these duvets
              of molten grass
                    and a jury of seedheads.

A tree left
       from myth
              to mark the spot
                    our giants fell.

Site of Fairy Well, Carbis Bay

There is mischief here
in the form of broken brooches
and rusted pins. In quiet mind
a voice hums aspirations
and bolonjedh for the sands
of the withered child's house.

No Cottingley fairies, no cardboard
conspiracies. Just teylu
borne from shared padera
and padera and repeated prayer.
Turn back from the shore
and speak Kernewek out loud -

these ways turn dreams
into hourglasses.

St Levan Well

I.
puffinus
puffinus

II.
rock
sea and
rock sea
lavender

III.
thrift
clearwing

IV.
silver-
studded
blue

V.
pearl-
bordered
fritillary

VI.
humpback
whale

VII.
white-
beaked
dolphin

VIII.
roe deer
grey seal

IX.
red admirals
clouded yellows

X.
hawker
dragonfly

XI.
besides
st selevan's home

XII.
baptism water
salt water

XIII.
cure
insomnia

XIV.
cure
toothache

XV.
cure
eye disease

XVI.
overlooking
gentle beach

XVII.
a vision of
marine tourists

XVIII.
a splendour
of grass and hill

XIX.
subtle myth &
sublime cliff

XX.
glory of st
levan well

Ballowall Barrow

Here lie Borlase's cists
in tender sleep and sweet
embrace, urns and delicate
alterations of Carn Gluze.
The towering stack a monument
to generations of extinguished
candles, lights from a village
never set to waste the dark again.

Here the rubble of a funeral
march and the loss of anonymous
lives. The sum of their work
a trip to a museum in later
glory. In deep moats and
deeper chambers, the charred
ash too loose to tattoo
onto the crossed flag.

Here the landscape in retrograde,
a seagull's call to a beach picnic.
The excavation of rain clouds
and weaknesses left fossilised.
The last hundred moves forward
for time keeps digging cists.

Bosigran Cliff

Here, the anvil chorus
of the tide's broken shore,
and the threat of Mercury's path
across the granite climb
and drop.

The bow wall immersed
in dangerous identity
and the welcome
of historical inaccuracy.
The gull cries for silence
and the sailor waits
for uncertain seas.

Cape Cornwall

The dense sand at night
airs a sense of desperation
in heavy footsteps racing
to the ocean's door.

The gentle weeping
of shrews acts a dead
centre of the cape
held together by foam.

The back of a coffin
brings a reckless home
asleep in holes waiting
for the day to return.

Carn Galver

The
boulders
and
stones
are
lined
up
here
for
a
neolithic
age.

Chapel Euny

Upon
the
three
first
Wednesdays
in
May
find
the
healing
you
came
for

Chapel of St Levan

You can crack the world in two
by simply riding through St Levan's
stone astride a horse.

You can break everything apart,
and start again with a promise
to never baptise Johana.

You can find the green man
after the hollow threat of the black
death's resurgence has passed.

You can pay respects to the Khyber,
and try to determine the difference
between salt and shard.

You can hear the ship's bell sing
invisible through the night air,
and feel both calm and fear.

You can visit remains of one of
the county's oldest chapels, yet
still not feel at home.

Chûn Castle

The fort circled in tin protection,
a line of ancestry chasing
the Celtic Sea back at low tide.
Rows of pilgrims in loss
and undisputed glory determined
to bathe in acid soil,
a weight lifted in disembodied
soul and torn flesh.

Smelt the identity of perpetual
youth in better houses
than the bricks
of broken castles can give.

Kenidjack Cove

I.
American Redstart
Along this swollen path, there may
be small warblers plump on moth.
An immigrant from decidious trees,
at home in open canopy. Like the
insects it strikes, it is unlikely to see
the end of day, or watch the humid
summer bless the cove in warm mist.

II.
Snow Bunting
A snowflake in a county that rarely
welcomes sheets of white. A
disinterest in flight, except to leave the
damp spring for daffodils to enchant.
The Snow Bunting's song echoes across
Kenidjack in rare love on rarer days,
when the granite is soft under foot.

III.
Red Eyed Vireo
Olive green but visible only
through the sweet notes of tender
birdsong, the first of twenty
thousand. The babbling stream a
bath for quiet seasons. Sleep under a
warming sun, on the fork of a branch,
where the arsenic roams the valley.

Lanyon

Lynyeyn.
Liniein.
Leniein.
Lenien.
Linyeine.
Lenyen.
La-nine.
Lanyayn.
Lanine.
Lennyen.
Laneyn.

Portheras Cove

Though the fog has cleared -
        the sand a gentle approach -
                every shard and hazard
                        resists the lighthouse's call.

Though the time has passed –
        the shore paradise again –
                every wrecked memory
                        returns on the highest tide.

Sancreed Well

Step 1: Strip the clothing from your body and take the pain with it.

Step 2: Hang your rags from the tree and leave.

Step 3: As the seasons swell and change, your markers will begin to drift and fall.

Step 4: Dedicate this freedom to the saint of father killers. Let him carry you as swine over the threshold of the new world.

St Eunys Wshing Well

Into the well three times,
once each for the giant's call.
Summer stretches its branches
into the cold ache of the whistle
and the shrill call of the well's
broken iris.

The water still runs to the core
of the land's settled heart.
Hold firm for infirmity
and the rainfall of
deciduous settlements.
These mottled trees

reach for a black-crossed
heaven. Into the well three
times, once each for the call
of children left stranded
in a town built without sustenance
and left for the leisure of the rich.

Tregeseal East Stone Circle

Nineteen of the last hundred,
dancing as the lone part
of a depleted tripod.

All the granite girls
left to live the sabbath
in their clotted tombs.

Now a scratch for the cattle
to ring the ocean off
above the whipped tide.

A reminder of the aura
in trampled land,
and the love of dance.

Portals from the west
bring the last remnants
of a neolithic age.

Trendrine Hill

Trapped between the twin quoits
of Zennor
and Sperris,
in harmonious wreckage
of a past left to fend for itself.

The rubble points towards
twin towns
and undertows,
but never loosens its grip
on the lessons of preservation.

The tales are spun and rekindled
in chough
caught fingers,
where the death of identity
is paramount to economy.

Run across this hill in Easter winds,
wide lipped,
bug eyed,
and recognise the greatest asset
we have is to lose everything we had.

Veor Cove

Summer
does
not
bring
early
sand
or
high
water,
just
the
beach.

St Helen's Oratory

Even the crosses have been replaced with leftovers found in nearby fields, less relevant than before. The well has had it's share of tempers and tempest's stone, in rage the future has lost sight of reason.

There, upon the sun 'Τούτῳ Νίκα' and an etching into the wrong rock.

Chapel Euny

Upon the three first Wednesdays in May find the healing you came for.

Gurnard's Head

Not so much a fish
but a lover's quarrel
or a broken-hearted
tryst against the rocks,
spines pressed into
the swollen tide.

Leak into the scrub
and melt into the sea.

Everything within
reach named after
the reason Cornish
men have nothing
left to do, but roam
the wild world o'er.

Site of Holy Well Morvah

The things we love the most are the things we lost and rediscovered.

Near St Just

A.
Here the road ends in blanket fields and lost cattle.
Gather your wits and turn back.

B.
Here the road begins in quilted land and mapped cattle.
Gather your strength and forge on.

Blood Fjørd '89

2019

Sjálfside for the Guðless

Happingja is not victory,
nail me to the birdhús and
let fjöævuhs thrive on me.

If Guðson deyd for me
he wasted a gunoise at martvottur,
why would he dey for apathy?

Krossdeath at night I am heimless.

Pikatrapp

Maykä my mind keeps this in husk
because we are kytkettound
regardless of distance
        and while I

now know this to be vääryys on varying
tasotrapps, you hold my kvíðiangstf
like a lapsi holding tight
        to vagga.

Petal

Ruðinbløð hue, only matched
by nonnífsøl – filtered
through some myndkuva
program – shima across
the gnowee nonsömn muscle
contorting forms of
happiside across my face. In
kausøl to come I will only

be nedulaa of the petals
that letfaramentea, crashing
to the bølevenn of a cardiac
arrest. I lokk the skjárslátt
níf between my örvraw'd
fingers and try to pensjieve
align them, armed with
good åsundur and a poor

librasaga of papiyon – at best.
They työnsiov an arc of ósæð,
when I awake with a huomaamatonsað
smile, but every time the kausøl
hiukkrin and the petals drift bannaðira.

Sömn

If I could lokk my øye
long enough to make
the punkxel
kadöutt
and the maa seep out
like the níf of a regnbåw
leaking into the valtantíkk,
I'd häfttack my lokkøye
and kross for sömn
to calcify my tæårrs

Sølregnbåw

The best sølregnbåw
    float
            unaided
                    hiukkrin by

sugar noter and a small plus sign.
A reason to kill djöfaðirullin,
to march with the angels
and hang anttevaltti banners
from the horns of fallen
taatto.

Hlöökhe

Crestfallen and ündderbåt
the heilólå to my suulöngu was met
by words kytkettound to geist happingja
which fails to bortdrömn the dauðrann to breathe.

The rich lapsi believes my gull moments are lunamåne,
as if hjartslátt is a strength to accentuate,
as if tracing my blød onto noter isn't inblød enough,
as if my weaknesses are a væist best served on stolen china.

I am fjöævuh in words and bordering on kross-parody
in a maa where my self is a geist drawn in noterblød.
The rich lapsi dug his notertrunk into my Rorschach mess
and gave my djöfaðirullin a poesistö.

Huomaamatonsað

Hús húsk pikatrapp.
Krosstrapp, pikkakross.
Hús húsk vagga, opaali.

Örvraw væist.

Nonöwllwö möllöm

Nonsøl heimless
hiukkrin øye, øyris,
lokkøye.

Djöfaðirullin –
djömoðirulin –
pikatrapp.

nonvikkract tørf,
blødfjørd '89,
02kausøl89.

nonöwllwö möllöm
haek. Kross death
krossdeath.

Injsaður

Katolik theüörie, maapmaap heimurrin guð.
Himiníf sjóndeildarhnífuringur /
himiníf åightsølsprakk /
himiníf unpipydin.

Spinn mai bassklav, trebklav, bedrúm.
concenkittää ckord cündderbåt /
concenkittää ckord övvurbåt /
concenkittää ckord båt.

Inblød húsk disclottinjurdd krossøl.
Jubilariemu jikuaivos /
jubilariemu jiku /
jubilariemu.

Regnbåw Nästikk

I see you in valtantíkk.
You are pearløst
and gull
in ways that abandon Guð's architecture.

You are the lunamåne
to every distrakskijöitä
my trunk has made,
and all we do is sort nästikk
by regnbåw.

Flat Heimurinn

If I had to choose a katolik theory
it'd be flat heimurinn,
so you and I could dangle our legs into himiníf
and repeat our vows among the åightsølsprakk

but we'll have to make do with åight
to løpemaap the curvature of maa
together
as we spinn on an axis
for our first mai.

SHITSHOW

2020

Psykos/*((Girlyas))*

I'm alone on the western front,
again,

I'm handcuffed to the shore
and I launch myself into
work. It won't

be long, gunslinger, won't be
years before the minotaur chorus
[we're the chorus, the slender
minotaur]

wounds.   You w/o me & us converging
                                 let us speak, let us, let us, let
                                 us

        speak plot.

Peninsula, you're cap smoke to the
right temple, it's early

easy morning. Operator, we only
phone the wrong numbers. My
daughter speaks in keys

now and she ain't & she is. And
you ain't. You certainly ain't.

Bone Idol

I've never set foot in a pub without
boxing gloves and a can of socialism –
they wanna split us by those who down
pints and those that quaff – the working
class is a rainbow is a taught violence –
I've never set foot in a pub without a
reason to vote – a terraced house tory is
still a tory – a terraced house terrorist is a
consequence of an iron fist – it takes a
parliament to kill a dream and the daily
mail to kill a kid – I've never crossed a
picket line I didn't love –
environmentalism is for the rich I sustain
myself on pesticides – we've got slide
tackles in our veins and yellow carded
kids – thatcher killed my granddad we
dream of feeding her asbestos – we've got
community and a fried breakfast – put the
kettle on – round 2 and no
longer sparring – I've never loved a tory
and I don't plan on going home

Aaron Dean

Look, the first step is to take the pension, shimmy it
Under your waistcoat while the vultures circle the
Watercooler; they ain't interested in your petty

Theft, o snow-driven vulture. The key is in the star
Signs, sheriff, in the way you present yourself.
The brave boys in blue bellowing obscenities out

The window watching whistling waves of threats
And a handgun shaking. You can hold a protest
In your own house if you got markers and a spitRoast piggie

polyps – they ain't the hurting kind,
The real stomp your skull like a grapefruit freshly
Soured good morning world today is a lovely day to

Notice how your hand trembles, how your knees
Shiver in Spring, how the sirens scream 'BEAT RAW
BEAT RAW BEAT RAW.' You're always one

Cheque short of a full bank statement short of a
Story shared while pilfering the evidence lockers
Of angel dust, ket, the strong stuff that keeps a perp

Cigarette burnt the time it takes to grow and heal
A tumour, a festering wound. Take the pension, hit
Them where it hurts, then spend the cash on a

Decent pair of gloves, a balaclava, and a silencer.
Cops love fingerprints, they collect them and
Store our differences. Keep yours to yourself.

Herlin-Bamlet

Light water graphite
sarcophagus; pacification
      of red, burns intra
-damp, it is late enough for dusk
      to stain you again,
      you are too young
to shed thyroid – we hoard bananas
forecast corrosion / body heat mummifies
summer, stings fulcrum pivot fulcrum.
      I'm twice melatonin;
circadin-bred pensionable sleep
abstinence / swaddle in rock
      armour – dressed
Blayais (
success is not knowing the names
of four bad crows). Curriculum skills
by the light of the silvery moon, a
physicist; I love you calling them 'the
dips' – 'bluebell woods', I 'the resevoir'
      left gleaming backpack
Thursday / legacy box. Approaching,
      I will outlive myself,
      you pipsqueak.

Snow Smear

You and I -- spread -- wafer thin
across hollow prism needles,
I love you with low visibility;
a pack of thermal gloves and

glow sticks. The banks are lit up
like bioluminescence at a wedding
or that baby bump glow
before the life change, here we

melt in time; torn I quit bleeding
so springtails may replace my
nervous system with an itch
so splendid it causes

us to tear off my skin
and cook it on the campfire. You
see, this is love: us eating my
flesh under platelet dark clouds

Contingency Plan: Red Circles (Ophelia)

Ivory sinks the plum's flesh into the gate
of heaven, weakness is present in every
　　inch of the cheek. She has a foxes cry
　　　　　　and crime to frost in the parlour, we
never call it the parlour, but I do ask parlez-vouz
　　Francais? Her tongue is undone by a run
of weak spots and sun spots in antithesis of
　　　　　　dialogue, and it's no wonder
she truly speaks fox. The weight of heirlooms
　　we can never offer because we can
never offer, because we can never stop
　　　　　　collecting junk in the hope it means
　　　something. I am holding her first tooth
and you are present with anaesthetic.

Small, Wingless

I was born on a two piece
pay later, an interest
rate dictated by my
birth centile. I was breeched
in instalments, spread
across the year; my mother

birthed an overdraft limit,
christened the mass in
common tongue. Learnt
to make space a premium,
notched into the damp
like a silverfish pedalling

into the core of us. My
mother's loss in the plaster-
board shaped like every
pet we begged to need
us. My father counting
grief in a shell in the roof,

      the difference between
      me and a mortgage
      is that gutting a house
      takes time.

Levant 1919

Other materials, even in iron
pressed fatigue. The calm
precedes the storm precedes sleep
stretched so thin it is broken
in twilight. Home is void by work,
miners are void by pattern.

Full of intent, patterns
of populace against iron
for the sake of cheap work.
Cracks spread across calm
chatter, the bulk of broken
beams turn'd loose in sleep,

so deep to be eternal sleep.
Every timber leaves a pattern
neither confirmed nor broken
in the wake of the iron.
There is a permanent calm
with the permanent loss of work.

Choked by the need for work
in the palm of dead; sleep
as insurance against calm
infinity. the depth of patterns
in the onyx of an iron
wall. The rods are made to be broken

and rebuilt to be broken
again. Across the soiled work
tundra, run beneath iron
rain scalding the dreams; sleep
tonight in delicate pupils. Pattern
patchwork fields for the rest, calm

to be laid upon the sweet, calm
soil. Tin prices are made to be broken
and lost as prayers spread pattern
across a duchy sky. The end of work
and the frightful, long sleep
of an anxious walk to ruin. Iron

every calm friend lost to work
into all of the night's broken sleep.
Press their pattern deep with iron.

Melatonin Spring Collection

2020

Losing a Mandate;

Sealing kisses -
velvet of a harbour town,
are both Pallene
and Methone
fillings - stand.
Of giants
(myths against
the backdrops;
complete ring
of alkyonides,
the margins
matter, suspend
expectation and
nurture the heat)
irreplaceable

Kind of Blue of Blue

in blue.
i chalk patience on the kerb,
am allergenic   weighted in grass,
and sit

uncertain of sharing.

there are too many words.
- three quarters of them, alone,
describe my safe space:
where i duvet.

i reach

for the hoover and
with shattered glass,   probe
my newborn blister.
pick the scab;
always
on my knees as a child
my gums as an adult.

a specialty

meeting   arranged
to let the leaves settle into

a routine of infinity/infirmity.

Infatuation Model

Impact measures
the credibility of
both retinas. DAMN,
the child is sombre,
stretched

across the eternal
summer;
that dark alley
where yellow

meets the wounds
on bone fragment.
There are removals

from the air's
majestés. Oxygen
the tone of stretched
thin toilet paper.

Five acres of tepid
rainforest is strewn
across our dashboard,
and we cry for a
Father's approach.

Loose as the fuse box
we use for firewood.
Loose line the streets.

Dark Battalion Phosphorescence

You were a thousand
words / architects spreading
space to create grotesques /
left alone with / out a glass
and Hemingway dreamt of
manicured fingers / two
of them yours, neither /
trying to save the world
from / you / could have it /
there's no / time like the
bit about the Triomphant /
smashing victory in the
form / of a poem and a
veiled threat

Invasion (The Slow Fall / Imbalance / Fall)

she held the rock close
both eyes bruises in
than we had either ever
methods to kill the waxing

waited for seaweed
avoidance / three nuclear
across the tonal majors
weighed our shins with

rain dances for fertility in
and heights confirmed our
her knees and floated like a
with all the grace of a

longer than we deserved
warranted / the sun
we ate the souls of
of our spectres

Tides are the rise and fall of sea levels caused by the combined effects

You scratched the surface,
held oranges in
ethanol, apples groped   with

the rim of your
eyes.   'The sum of us
in frozen breeze. Our

[shimmered] length' to the nature's
cling, to the time repatriated.   .
Sheered the rug in our

torn terror.
We slipped   into sleep,
gossip, truce and

our psychology. Pair   of
signs, symbols,   of a love never
found at home, and   instead.

Contemporary Theft

Pearls made from rope and
hermit crabs – given
skulls as shells. You
drew prayer. Our bed was

a chair to the heralds weighted with
Saturn burnt into the edge.
Invites to the draught, rested
contemporaries. You glistened when,

and laughed when, thorns and a half
dozen roses left in the fuse box.
Moments and belief in the death
parade, the jubilee – you – yourself –

Melatonin Spring Collection

A fistful of
bone to dull
all four
snowmen
leaking coal,
onto our bodies
and swearing
sun. Turf burns
a compass in
portrait
and crop circles.
In the patch
decorated with whispers,
there are cyclists, or at least
a place
amongst wasted noises
capillaries. Stairways
for astronomers,
leaking into the gaps
and waiting – O

Origami Event Horizon

Sailor's hand-made
paper boat set
where the elephants

paper basket with
every note made
from a bonsai tree.

Edges of the
stratosphere collected
the last flight to

the moon. In a backpack
you held the-
meditative techniques

of eastern. Only you and
books, quotes from
you, sat, scarry-eyed.

To push you from
you, to wash you of
you from the edge of-

intermittent failure.
Keep your name on;
for silence to speak.

Catapults Are the Best Way to Smash Your Neighbour's Windows

diamonds
shaped as

the   tread of
rolled cigarette
ends down the hill   and counted
shrapnel
marking asbestos in   sculpted

in the shape   marches
excommunicated
protest signs

problems
of vaulted ceilings and the
gap in the window

friendship
into winter's grip

library road
collected the dresses   of every angel
building
a house the size of
sycamore seeds   in speechless

night streets screeched broken fights
squared

                        raised a ballet
dancer and waxed   hospital floors

pushed strays on
bikes away from
urtica dioica

excuse to breathe
their names when

our ties were
cut too close to our

windsor knots

took the

boxes when

in the bath holding a head

Written Prayers/Evangelical Basement Sale

Out of consciousness, moat water along those
seldom fought. Cotton soft edges,
promise to bring warmth, aurora,
stretches of terror.   There are colloquialisms

and resurrections. Microphone to gullet,
flesh for magpies to my mother,
for the diptera morning's mail.
Reminders of Cuban sweatshops, warheads

from the nitrous charts. Pond scum. Drought
        conditions, two polio-headlights. A turn
space into snapped twigs,
forced but polished - did we speak? Through

wartime, passed from, to, crushed. In lamb's
wool pulled over eyes.   A battering ram, the sleet
laid west over   responses to angels. All
angles and wasted evangelical basements.

We built a podium to counting a punch.

Priority I: Regent Stones

We never drink speech
in ornaments, instead we
sip gently at the
caps melting in
the northern hemisphere,
the southern
swarm   of wasps;
doom shaped peace.

The rifles are birds,
owls perched on
the crow's gift to
our territory
and tinnitus.

Broken metronomes
have robbed us of our home
to termites.
Mark them in blue.
We are the end of   an equation.

Still x
-armed God
is a variable;
an hour in a year in   Japan
in the most minimalist   zine.

It was beautiful.

You now sleep
          insomnia
          even and half,
waking nights.

Like puffins –
just like flamencos   look like toucans,
and you look tired
scratched out,

searching to start
a planet,
hidden sails and
          a window you turned away   from, chased.

To bring you water
and to find you,
warm, I kissed your   -   heavy hair.

The Time On Mneme, Jupiter

Felt your mist on the side,
swallowed spiders in dusk's

Halloween. Clouds are spun
from the letters you composed

with barbed wire fingers. Yet,
it is the phone in trepid step

and alien hours of you, determined
you, that exists in the grip of

nosferatu's stare. Sheets marking
wage slips fresh with the scent

broken and weeping. In the nebula
of *dead planets* – I bore the space

to stamp your threat

Space + Breathe

breathes hot rose sweetness, our summer air
presses against the   bowl of strawberries
& cold patches of midnight.
Before Nyx rises to the east of Venus, we are a light year
too young to quit from Hypnos   sleepy eyed & my lungs.
Globules have you   & us   screaming in unison.
I play to pump   – a dream organ –   into being.
Of shadowy figures; tonight I will dream,
who cartwheel premonitions
& poppies, of robot daughters.
I, catchers from every frame, have hung
father of darkness.   Old age is the
table reserved by the boatman amid the primary sin.
We caught our breath,   stopping our hearts
every time   we were too busy counting bubbles.

i lighthouse now

ice sheets melt in
nestled in the crook
of oblivion ink
of tokyo and
writes three symbols
spread the first a patch
second salt from edamame
the third your
angles at the foot
and to build shelter
light is a fluorescent beam
of a sled at winter
i lighthouse now you awake
the lookout for shipwrecks
cargo kept soundly
for fear of nightmares

Solipsistic Pessimism

The screw is another / wasted pivot / it is the interruption of
skin from winter's / front thigh. Diamonds are /as the iris lets /
and each minute is only as valuable / as the eventual / rotations
are perceived / among the roll of infant tongues. By the shape
/ to create experience trapped by desire / in heavy old wounds
which / slumber there and battle. These are the seas that hold
squid / angels, and wrecks the size of / never explore. It is more
solipsistic / than my / history should ever allow / to show / you
my cries, ad verbatim / and infinite.

Eyed: Tiger Moth

Sum of our weight in
miniatures, indifferent
to hobbies
(are movements
the shape and grace
of every
of dawn).

Prelude to the rest,
the opening
concerto dreams
compose in the misshapen
leftover morning.

The first cry
with eyes
bougainvillea
trimmed, and allergies
everything
from perfect.

Built a home to house
and a garden
to seed her
snowfall.

Hold Hungary: Priority 2 –
Research Proposal

Memories from,
shaped and soiled,
opaque frames in Hungary,
unable to shake hands

but through the
baggage in the star-sunk attic
leading to the light.
Stares and aging nests

blistered from asthmatic skin.
Your flesh is still
burning nails and lashes
for the creation of an

hour with tenderness
to leave the bedroom
(other than a knife
wound in stasis).

Cherished the white
room, a warm glow in
the worst parts of rain
(favourite summer dress).

Tension repeating the words
we sang when with/with
delta sleep.
You magnifying the

hand and the back of
torturous indigo-brushed rest.
The way the room
and the sun's music

die in the middle of
irrelevancy in the capital cities of
all the countries we
have argued in.

The beetle's hour as the-
oesophagus-
lack of return,
stories hushed and

leaning towards optimistic.
Blast of foam and glass;
öwllwö's tooth in serenity
drawing Anthe

under the bed as an
escape from domesticity
on the tulips we grew
a place for the cat to nap.

one-fifth are roughly spherical, but the majority are not spherically symmetric

This nebula of petals, this mint leaf tea planet,
this ambulance, this arc from library shimmer –.
locked these brothers' stories. I pinched the dirt with

broken fingers, I lived among the ants. A vacuum.
The tiniest places I knew existed in the borders/scars
in the back of Antarctica. Believed in cardiac arrests and

profiling the police/hypnotherapy. My wife was ill. I
panicked about false smiles and brushed the web I
long to catch my prazosin in, to blow the soil bloomed

in crimson butterflies the shape of Budapest. We held
snowflakes to our storm eyelids. We were the worst
parts of green and blue/or dead skin cells? Attempted

spectral - each postcode another notch in a tango romeo
one five (we had no car) two echo tango. Yes, human
because we can see art, ark and arc. Special was tiring was

barely family within broken tills hidden behind my flower
bed, my waste psychology. I cancelled memories. I ran
to the shade, spiders crunching through their mother,

out of somebody - even if that person wore your clothes
and your window met daylight and 'don't you think
it's nice to exist in the ice cream freezer in the cinema.'

Time – shades – grows into weeds/documentaries.
There is still a picture of empty space and geraniums in
my story/was/was not/my storm/was not/my swallow

away. We laid our lives out in photographs on the bedside,
I could count my victories on the eyes left behind. The web
you built has found   meaning from the little corner of teeth

in your mirror at night. My eye in the spaces where it wraps itself in coils around the back of my hand.

Harbour Equinox

2020

Minor Bones, Restructured

News perspective concerns advertisers,
          (it's ok)
      you are my relevant target audience
      – too surveyed; slush pile shush
           file away
slow news days are currency like familial love
      as daily representation (
oblivion one-on-one with the trash) our means
of love allow us to discredit. Favour
          my father's clone;
      I am melatonin symptom –
matrimonial channels
          wire/copy/disseminate:
      'Sterile surface – rebate costs of
wrapping
             shin & splint.'
Report back: minimal interest;
circadian rhythm bleed me dry: entranc'd
to first hearing, sharing is shaping
      is manipulating,
      strong-arm tactics are barbaric refuse.
If my family could see me now (hush,
the baby is asleep
      and you've been coaxing me
          feverish for twenty
minutes) could see familiarity now.
      Father is front
          page news,
      too old to be worth the novelty
      of breaking minor bones.
Ristretto every morning and Lysine
– convince myself awake
      and not a symptomatic lapse –
familiarity is intimacy and
      melatonin please bleed me
      dry.

Splendid Giants

The satellite is, you climbing all heights,
a kingfisher remarkable, alkyonides,
        disrupt the way i weight old
lined parchment in suicide doors (grief
transformation - herculean effervescent
        o, bleed us) castration and
flowery, it is, to wait, it is in our nature to

birth giants and provide watered graves.
The movement enamour'd is movement
        squared, weightless in envy,
envoy to empty colonies as eons settled
in dusk at the rise, great rise among the
        crest of blue-black oil sweat labour
each bird a lake and reason. We, Semipalatinsk,

semi-panicking our patois useless among
stars who speak treble clef in frequencies
        designed for fishermen's temporal
lobes; lines cast across event horizons, her
eyes upon the grace of eternity, eternal,
        eternity the width of dream anthe
stretch swung, to become a bird is better

than to drown in ice. Shivered swollen burnt
nodules (we have self-immolated). Initial
        free form takes shape stolen –
across dust is the same – love through
commodities through common oddities as
        capital stretch light years across hotels
stationed, communities as global enterprise

and us following rules we swore to abandon
on home. The shrine maiden of the kingfisher
        of your knight who is the fantasy
of the alkyonide festival on the coast of

hourglass; moon-heavy skies pluralised
elimination of champagne blesses
the atom's Earthly wave kiss (the baby

narrows) typical and jealous – the following
watering in the evening is heavy blessed
the baby moon's nuclear packs.
Winged giant, splendid, battling Athena,
token gestures the size of multiple universes
sacrificing offspring for just the
one rock to scale mountains for legislation.

Night Shining

Hibakusha epicentre blurring a-bomb
cataracts; intercellular vision crater
where the baby kicks
                              the white side of
a moon's nocturne-gaping wound
mediated on the microcephaly impact
skull;
        weight and size is typical in torturous
hypnogogic crossroads supersede one short
of diagonal trace – plate batteries in
                                        second-
hand toys sing kilohertz. Cork pop both
slosh red in wine and dark in muscle
memory counting shapes on cloud formation;
thicker sacrificial lambs,
                        noctilucent
                                        during
twilight's late moon-heavy sky burden songs.
Heliocentric termination of effervescent
rapidity blesses the kiss of atom ground wave,
sharp; dense
                quartz – strontium stroma strobe.

172

Pyrocumulonimbus

Somewhere above all of above in
collapse heat vector skin cells we
shed; I love this – love you radiant
      between troposphere and
      high stratosphere; here too
      over us we burn through
ourselves, release you I energy store
cataclysm catalyst architecturally
dissipated flammagenitus drench
      each other in sleep turn
      twist limbs – I will wait
      for your arms to be my
chain-reacting critical mass crater,
reminiscent: low level Castle Bravo.
You, I, and us spread thin among
      Chupadera Mesa; beta
      burns flesh bath-scorch
      hair teases goosebumps-
internal war bled pyrocumulus
nocturnal moksha further gleam
our bruise; I leave myself behind
      personal me / Ashima /
      upper stratosphere
      caste meditation drone
spiral – I love you, again, you decide
to drop multi-armed forms - beget
a white dwarf stained yellow.

Cervidae in Cortona

crown and cup hunt
grand-orgue montre through
clarion more so than
saint sulpice /
                    the virgin of
the star sailors bless bez smaller
than void switch for rut
marred 'neath /
                    adored by angels

        adored by angels whence
transparent propaganda lusts
cul-de-four vault /
                    violently
silent mouth te deum
and christus upon the
shed of winter coats
christening tree and pew
orgelbewegung hymn drag
swell /
        box

    box press antler shed
werkprinzip the sweet blessed
congregation of rutting smack
antler press breed /
                    calcant
calcify hoof prints tithe stop
the weight solitary clamp as
constant pressure in /
                    windchests

        windchests

Inedia

The swollen breast of sweat
odor; either flower blooms
strongest mark, death stretch
damp breath to linger on the

Seraph's conclusion, when
the soul bears no stain, crown
of thorns on Ferron in sleep
and grace for acetone ketosis

in itiriti snake's grasp, high
angels, low angles, neither bear
marks bore upon brand-burnt
bodies of the late shame;

corruptible lamentations.
The single point object into
the single point image crimson
lent period waste, we lie

awake and cross our arms over
the impact and learn to love the
science of resolutions.

Lunar Eclipse, Harbour Equinox

During sleep,
our fossil body sleeps during sleep,
I love you side by side.
Lay the fossils down.
I'm sorry. Show mercy,
lie, lie, lie down. Sleep.
Prepare to feed our soul.
Heal, jump us, moor, far.
I hear the heavens are empty.
Be a complete moon, here.
Lie-and-Hold-to-Lie, sleep. Sleep.
Prepare to feed our soul.
Heal, jump, distance, moor.
It bleeds me, the heavens are empty.
Be full of moon, here.

(I'm delaying, I'm delaying)

Lying, holding, sleeping. Sleep.
Prepare to feed the soul.
Healing, depth, distance.
He washed me; the heavens are empty.
Fill the moon, here.

In Breach of His Windpipe

The pantheon is split / rimate minimum
wage legislation, if I am an immigrant
you are the land I have come to love as

Marduk to power and divination;
aquarius struck solely state intervention
as free-market criticisms of invisibility.

If we see the thunderbolt we can proclaim
lightning, but otherwise is to, in fairness,
lost love awaiting, coward, call forward

Sarpanit. New years bring new reasons,
twilight rendered obsolete by the rising
moon and you breastfeeding our child

as latched to the waking sun. You seal me
up in parcel paper / hoard Rhea beneath
Ceres in the Pampas threatened with decay

(radioactive) and the worship of
tambourine and drum up loss
incensed in community; your milk

is never free to break, even when lunar
cycles are counted on both hands with
those sat beside mother in half-life.

Perfectly Reasonable Justifications
for Nuclear Apocalypse

2020

White Sails Withdrawn

Slow-wave sailing by delitescent
as cable length tethered,
ground, to waist, keep grip
asunder dependent
sleep navigation and range
swapping in night
shining permutations. Us
contradistinguished
neonatal swaddled within
swaddle you Aegean;
strained upright throughout
sharing with oceanic
Gods, submerging weapons
beneath pillow to force
kinship from broken clay;
await the good reason
to silently drown ourselves

Herlin-Bamlet

Light water graphite
sarcophagus; pacification
          of red, burns intra
-damp, it is late enough for dusk
          to stain you again,
          you are too young
to shed thyroid – we hoard bananas
forecast corrosion / body heat mummifies
summer, stings fulcrum pivot fulcrum.
          I'm twice melatonin;
circadin-bred pensionable sleep
abstinence / swaddle in rock
          armour – dressed
Blayais (
success is not knowing the names
of four bad crows). Curriculum skills
by the light of the silvery moon, a
physicist; I love you calling them 'the
dips' – 'bluebell woods', I 'the resevoir'
          left gleaming backpack
Thursday / legacy box. Approaching,
          I will outlive myself,
          you pipsqueak.

Sileadh e a-nis

neither integrated crackle the mean
house a sauna considered burning
bonfire's spirited teine biorach
heat torn clothes in the uidh
without those things kids wear
blister prone arm float safety
trapped valley clear rock formations
like thunder striking two

cloud partition stone mazes
curtain pull vocal cords flash
translucent eat exhausted circles
used / remove ordinary species
resentful nature of sleep brisk
distend kettle whistle
breaking swollen internal hope
of a stove high-pitched contusion

eyelid the wasted shape-shifting
dynamics of a grasp of gravity
area geometric earth's crust
pull of thunder we mow clean heavy
white noise heaven-sent dirt into
confusion spread across restless
scars and sonder driver frictioning
brings more of the hypothalamus

EVERY CAVE HAS A WEDDING PARTY

If heart clave, sterile, blood,
foam and autoclave, know
there – valves pulsating
barosii, I warrant. Wipe
shelf from sure memetic-
free offspring. Encephalon.
You find a moon, no dark.

High Developmental Unconsciousness

spiritual polarity) from the west;
        determined irrelevant
by karmic cycles – jiva escapes,
        is reborn to escape
, you know this as Jung does
        (autonomous stock
images) and lectures both taboo
        through totem
chapter through verse – we inherit
        her persona as archetype
of the coffin-makers making millionaires
        of us all; incense
the choir – pass the night as hummingbirds
        know nectar from gestation
, you know primordial and spiritual
        enough to stop
calling his name; stone has nailed shut
        and prevented return
(expect new blessings – opposites in

Defect Coma

built-in incorrectly the steps misspelled
suggest you watch your alternative
words next to my name Aaron and another

Aaron then three possible keys followed by
a beep displayed prior to the return key
typing on one page press popular not my

view what words you show on and you
spell spelled line made most with word
beep character can be right to return type

when will spacebar press return type
more like kitten press when words to the
code can automatically backspace anywhere

after some sounds spelled please
return press other some type word
on anywhere and see please you

My Soul, My Left Hand, My Soul

Effigy. I'm a morbid love in my dress, a silent
prayer, so kiss me like our tongues are clean
clouds. This sweet death, divert my soul, your

stare promises infinite to radiate the effigy.
Beautiful clouds of death near you.
What sweet audio, a prayer in silence, your stare

promises and promises infinite. The Clouds.
Leave my morbid death, divert my soul, divert
my soul for promises infinite, take My Love, My

Torrent, My Covenants, and My Covenants.
Prayer beans have long been recited.
Cloud formation and the promise of immortality.

The Effigy. Leave my sweet love, leave my slit
throat, your stare promises infinite. Rest my blessed
sleep, a silent prayer, a silent prayer when you stare.

I will lean in tongues with their hearts as clouds.
It looks like the most promising door. Happiness is always
there when you want to sleep or walk in peace.

Sound in my heart, I speak like a cloud

Telescopal

Catholic children sung
        choir of angels raise
degloved flesh at molecular
        confession / miss

life bread without wine
        / resentful sleep
an eddy stripped raw
        sanctuary to rancid

saints / spore reproduction
        lends itself to
law being crushed epi-
        / pen / centre

hhhh hhhh hhhh

onyx on wasted sea gentle promises
parched against vivacity reminds
of tangents catecholamine
the size of papercuts sung mounted

lips this could be *the* tallest cliffs
where every line is across bristled
inverted *u* clear crystals
bring flowers from covered

oyster wine-dark spaces of sweat
windmills leap to bloom each
others and Ino's dearest dreams
in which we endophenotype sleep

God is a Builder

Innocent blood sashays
flood down the silence,
the grand silence

> *(I sung a prayer*
> *for loosened days)*

lost and vast
confession booth is
our boulevard captain;

solar eclipse, too.
Revere – celebrate
there's a vowel late

enchanted in terraces
there's blood diamond
ferris wheel work

> (?)
> *(fair work)*

bloodied? Swimming pool
in dark for fairness sake
party kiss, cost and tell

told, reservoir looming
hand weaving a dinner
knife [cut you full]

> *and here I am.*

all these hearts sticking
Il y a les vivants
And me, I'm in the sea.

Black Tie, Gold Bow.

The rainy season is vast,
the Spread of Heaven. Heat stress.
Unused metaphors:
black fever, gold arrow.

I cut my blood, cut my blood,
at the end of the golden hour, tap my muscle.
Unused metaphors:
black fever, golden arrow.

The air of the heavens extends the westerly winter
by expanding the sky's milk.
Unused metaphors:
black fever, golden arrows.

He gave them all to die again.

Swan River Daisies

Fell in love with the phone, the night
is raging and the waves are scattered
across both beds. Rainier Green
is amazing even under the underlying

moonlight where the swans run and her
lambs are thrown away just like the
bottom of water. Send the weight
of the sky from the sky; fear of in-home,

when the angels improve fields in harmonious
red colour with bright appearance. Galaxies
inspire us - sleeve matting for soft bed,
soft rest in rest with great strength falling

in Faith. In the thick of day, fog of
rain like weakness, it is powerful
light (such as visible parts such as the
brain, such as roads blocked by hard

logic). Warning of fire: cold for bones,
salvation is unknown. There is hope of
snow in the morning on the evening of
night, pencil-strong fog, hungry light

summer breeze, we will travel; have
breathing power. He will still look
beyond you (daylight does not work)
on the Cristal night. Genealogy,

the deep recesses, my soul to
the fallen black stone). Call light
into forest. A shocked boy, there
is injustice in animosity. Their

hearts are full of energy, keep in love
with this. Every planet changes below,
for you have found the heavens, your
love has been left on Earth. Unwelcome.

Manic dreams are becoming.

Humans are becoming a dream.
People are circling.

The evening was a thorn
on the Andaman Mountain trip,

at the peak of Oedad.
The evening was a thorn,

silence. Be calm, touch easily.
The evening was a thorn,

no one can guide us
Night Officer -

we'll import the backup.
People are inactive,

we're back.

It Was a Sacred Death

Stop all trees at the polar groove -
       I'll break my divinity,
       head my head,
       and reunite the people.
I do not drink my hair,
my father is coming over.
Gold is heavier in gold.
       Check my coils,
my sealant shakes Anthe magnetic tube,
My Package Mahman-Mathematical Hub,
the nuclear flux is found in retreat.
       Across all metrics;
dead bodies of dead bodies and golden sneakers -
       blue protection.
       Overall Dimensions,
       Cellular Estimates,
       I am a neighbour.
       I am a neighbor.
Colour in the walls of a house,
catch and disassemble the lowest notes.
Hold down the small note and drop it.
Stop all the trees on high –
I'm disgusted in my room.

The Afterlife of Pablo

Uncollected

Ultralight Beam

This beam, ultralight, Sunday depression;
my faith is a dream I persecute my
parents' holy war. Little light of mine,
I will deliver you serenity,

peace, loving, everything. Never going
to fail my child's blessing – home again.
I'm looking for a rainbow in the night
for the devils' first hallelujah. You

need your name, you feel your pain, my daughter,
damn, you end my holy war. I speak hell
to shield your name and pray for raincoats; look
for strength, glory be to Sunday. You can

never go too far when you can't pray for
an ultralight beam. This is a God dream.

Father Stretch My Hands Pt. 1

You're liberated, my only morning.
Your eyes remind me, I want to wake up
under your skin – nothing instigated.
This high model sun like you, beautiful.

You're liberated, my only morning.
I know you from the only power I
feel in my eyes. Looking like I'm gon' shoot
you, I feel liberated, say nothing.

You're liberated, my only morning
in Tribeca, when I don't even want
to talk to you. If I'm unwanted, you're
the power, the sun, that can wake me up.

You're liberated, my only morning
and now if I get bleach on my T-shirt⊠

Pt. 2

How do I kill you on camera, phantom?
I'll be taking licks, my father hurt my
soul; Momma lost control in the morning.
My back was broke, my jaw was broke, control

my hands and stretch that life round town. Killas
in Atlanta 'member me, my father,
like driving fast – crashed the ship on camera.
Twisting, phantom, twisting, time is lost I

miss you bad like a hundred hammers. How
do I bind to you, turn to you, find you
in the morning? I dreamed you understand
me like I'm a hundred killers taking

control. If you ask what my problem is
called, I just wanna feel liberated.

Famous

From the very start let us act famous
in the streets, in this hood, in the sky.
In the air over the sun, I can't try
to understand how to be free; nameless.

We ain't know we never Kanye famous
with personal debt, that day parade vibe.
Last month I wanted to wake up and die -
we way too late to be never nameless.

I love my girl in the air like a jet,
no matter why, we still wanted to see
free love, everybody hands over debt.
My own kin know me best, better than me.

Bam, a real estate agent, fresh to let.
Bam, you can't stop us wanting to be free.

Feedback

I made a jacket when sleeping, wake up.
I need a Gotham costume, the fabric
paper, the fabric cotton. I shouldn't
bother just doing what the cops taught us.

PETA got fashion: my father and a
Rottweiler – my mind been on snooze a long
time, my mind been on snooze for the wrong time.
Follow the motto: what the cops taught us.

Money never made the news, driving hands
up, I been wilder; these people ain't play
me. Even if my money low, crazy;
Steve Jobs, Steve Austin; what the cops taught us.

These good people mad genius: Hov, Oprah,
Jordan, Rodman, Pac, then the cops shot us.

Low Lights

some day the blue sky will open up a
testimony crying free accepted
the night wide in the middle with my heart
wondering how to guide me through the day

i love you with my life my body my
soul because bone matter arms how im now
anybody loved so good lord so free
my name will be blue these tears will be blue

my heart will be accepted guide me in
the middle of the night crying thank you
crying the life of day and open wide
some day the blue sky will open up a

testimony crying free accepted
some day the blue sky will love my body

Highlights

I wish my friends would die; paradigm shift
in video, slo-mo Christian – killed
equinox. I'mma marathon freak lord,
open my head, mama, amateur talk

lit the city; you want advice? God ain't
rich, he just got the highlights, superstar
pro. Walkin', livin', breathin' family
ain't my problem, he hit first, tell mama

I'm in the trenches like an idiot,
makin' one night my whole life every
time. I'm friends with wishin' I die, till I'm
livin' life with my girl and my baby.

I need my mama up in equinox.
I need to know if you my past or not.

Freestyle 4

What if we fucked on the dinner table?
What if we fucked on the dinner table?
What if we fucked on the dinner table?
What if we fucked on the dinner table?

What if we fucked on the dinner table?
What if we fucked on the dinner table?
What if we fucked on the dinner table?
What if we fucked on the dinner table?

What if we fucked on the dinner table?
What if we fucked on the dinner table?
What if we fucked on the dinner table?
What if we fucked on the dinner table?

What if we fucked on the dinner table?
Would everybody fuck on the table?

I Love Kanye

I love Kanye. Kanye in pink polo,
Kanye in the news, always sweet Kanye.
The man hate Kanye, the man always rude
to Kanye. Kanye chop up all the soul

and set on his goals, always sweet Kanye.
I love the new Kanye, I love the old
Kanye, I miss the new Kanye, I miss
the old Kanye. I always was Kanye,

and always be Kanye; bad mood, rude, news
Kanye. Straight from the go I love Kanye,
if Kanye made a song I love the beats.
Always sweet Kanye. Kanye invented

Kanye. I love Kanye like Kanye loves
Kanye, Kanye loves Kanye like Kanye.

Waves

I ain't scared to set the night on fire,
I ain't scared to set the cage on fire.
Waves don't die like bird don't die, baby I
don't die. Let me crash in to a fistfight,

that's just me, even when I don't need to
own the night, I crash. I don't fly; I don't
lie; I don't die. I wanna see if the
sun shine on you in the morning, if it

shine on me in the shade, in the night. Turn
me up, turn me away, I'm still gon' be
here, no lie, when the waves die. I don't like
to be the one for the moment if I

can be the one here in the morning and
night. I'm the one to set you on fire.

FML

I've been given a vision, a mission
to pour out my soul when you mention my
children. Remember nothing so I can't
jeopardize the layers of my life. I

love your voice, your self-control, through the veil
you fuck me one last time. Only I can
limit this episode and test the end
to all I've been given, revealing my

code to you; crazier than a minute
in control. The last time I would forget
my children, I'mma cause hell – don't test me.
The Lexapro store don't throw me nothing

before I pour out my feelings. Life's a
laugh for a minute, life's waiting to end.

Real Friends

How many deadbeat family fuck up
the church? Communion reunions, crazy
on free wine – they get what they deserve. I
ain't just blamin' the media, but I'm

blamin' centuries of 'what the fuck we
doin'?' The last time I remembered my
family I was defendin' a real
enemy – throwed dirt on my name; wasn't

finished. I ain't got kin, I got pressure,
I got nothin' on my streets. I guess I
got what I deserved; young daughter, one on
the way, real family I trust – forgot

how many extended, make time for real
family, immediate family.

Wolves

i have took
the sandwich
that was in
the fridge

and that
you were
hustlin'
for tea

i'm sorry
it was unseasoned
so burned
and so warm

Frank's Track/Siiiiiiiilver Surffffeeeeer Intermission

The energy in the town, in the big
tsunami already mixed official
wave. It's love, it's honor, it's wavey. All
life is precious, we found all the rings with

a cave in, the love and support we found
is precious. Burn out the heat and the light,
checking the fleshed out wave, the energy
in this game. I appreciate the wave

you keep in blackened rings. You. Just doing
you. Keep it loopy. Keep it wavey. We
ain't got no problem with no light and no
heat, the wave is here to do something big.

All life is precious. Max B and Yeezy
keep it wavey. Life is a precious wave.

30 Hours

I remember drivin' you back western
in the morning with no job like mom and
dad, now private school, gym, kids, families;
my life is like a movie – beginning,

middle, and end, I made myself happy.
I was in college, no life, no house, beams
not ultralight, renovations to my-
self. The best years were blurry like a drunk

pyramid; rise. My ex realise my
best version of her was me all alone.
I pictured you, my idea of a good
relationship: all love, no damages.

Western: we been drivin' 30 hours,
only thing open: my idea of you.

No More Parties in LA

I'mma shit poet, uninspired, my
confidence in regularly weak, lame
content don't add up. Miracles released
my repertoire, proper community

don't want a rookie – too soft, too selfish.
The next generation of writers got
plans, came here to get spiritual, promote
every direction. I'm regularly

threatened by my block, and worried 'bout my
daughter, my psychiatrist told me my
problem is the big disconnect from my
father; with mercy he will not hurt

me. I kill my movie, threatened by my
bulletproof intents. Every day poet.

Facts (Charlie Heat Version)

dirt grime filth over-reckless aggressive
infrastructure boom just like arrogant
designers made a million a minute
forget election cheating stealing why

never lifetime dropped the message extra
production hottest discussion numbers
accomplished nothin' pure luxury like
thick news deep news blessed to be alive news

employees slaves copped platinum trending
celebrate truth appraised talk jumped over
roots runnin' budget perfect days money
rodeo picture Yeezy house inside

hotel Adidas copped 2020
bring family home look how far we are

Fade

Your love is real / Ain't nobody fadin' /
When I think you gone / Ain't nobody fadin' /
You know better / Ain't nobody fadin' /
I feel hurt inside / I gone fade away /

Hold the middle so far / Ain't nobody /
Hold the boat 'til the whole / Ain't nobody /
Hold the whole world so far / Ain't nobody /
Hold the deep down / Ain't nobody fadin' /

I've been fadin' away / Nobody fade /
Your love is the whole world / Ain't nobody /
I've been fadin' away / Nobody fade /
Your love is the whole world / I fade away /

Deep inside / Down inside / I've been fadin' /
Down inside / Deep inside / You fade away /

Saint Pablo

Father I'm out of control, I know your
truth is: I'm not visible to you - but
I'm just pretendin' I can see the light.
Confirmation of your footsteps when I'm

crazy on Twitter, is in the night sky.
Your light was influential, family;
brothers down with your mission at home with
my folks – I'm the only one not on your

beams. Please speak to me, say somethin' before
I leave, I wonder where you are, father:
modern day God, scary to see, beaten
to submission and I'm fine now, I guess.

My wife knows my truth, that she visible
to me, her and my kid in the night sky.

Regulating the Nightwatch

Uncollected

Daniel Panteleo

You can crack a cop's head open with
An ice cream scoop if you run it under
Hot water first. Strip him down to his
Fleshy tendons, render his instincts

Silent. Pig's blood ain't much good
As a deterrent when you're ankle deep
In the trough blocking out a path home.
The watchmen don't eat doughnuts;

It's a lure, a false sympathy. Sugared
Up coked up waffle irons laughing
Into their shrapnel, their blood splatter,
Their chocolate sprinkle and coffee

White two sugars. You can kneecap
A boy in blue using a crowbar and
Some elbow grease, use the badge
To pop the patella out. He'll scream

But if you've done it right he'll feel
Every single step from the court-
House to desk duty to freedom to
The weight of an innocent plea.

Aaron Dean

Look, the first step is to take the pension, shimmy it
Under your waistcoat while the vultures circle the
Watercooler; they ain't interested in your petty

Theft, o snow-driven vulture. The key is in the star
Signs, sheriff, in the way you present yourself.
The brave boys in blue bellowing obscenities out

The window watching whistling waves of threats
And a handgun shaking. You can hold a protest
In your own house if you got markers and a spit-

Roast piggie polyps – they ain't the hurting kind,
The real stomp your skull like a grapefruit freshly
Soured good morning world today is a lovely day to

Notice how your hand trembles, how your knees
Shiver in Spring, how the sirens scream 'BEAT RAW
BEAT RAW BEAT RAW' You're always one

Cheque short of a full bank statement short of a
Story shared while pilfering the evidence lockers
Of angel dust, ket, the strong stuff that keeps a perp

Cigarette burnt the time it takes to grow and heal
A tumour, a festering wound. Take the pension, hit
Them where it hurts, then spend the cash on a

Decent pair of gloves, a balaclava, and a silencer.
Cops love fingerprints, they collect them and
Store our differences. Keep yours to yourself.

Paul Koester

Kill the fathers first, the gaudy seed
Bearers. Shovel road salt down their
Gobs until they vomit up their form

Of contraception. Preference

For *whatever gets the job done*:
Baton, stick, fist, knife, gun.
A swift kick like birds flocking

Laces tied   animal dominance.
Like cracking an egg like cracking

A head like peeling the scalp from
The back of the fur lined skull
And oozing flamingo milk from
Teat to teeth to tongue to kerb.

       When they sleep they dream of their sons,
       Dressed to the nines, sharp as razorblades
       In platform shoes, blitzkrieging

Major arteries. The struggle
Of fatherhood is in making
Breakfast when your kid is out
Unchecked.

       Put the dads
Out of their misery, the late night
Chat show host fathers making
Conversation, skirting around the edge
Of the nest like a murmuration to
The eve of comfort zones.   *Flog.*

The night-watchmen raise night-watchmen
But who razes the retirees, the gaudy, the
Salt-stuffed sandmen.

      Steal their TV sets and cardboard feed
      Them the news,   the insipid slant
      Of their spunk worming towards a good
      Battering – hand

Shandy and all the scalpels a cop can take
to the chest before daddy fries 'em up in
A griddle. Kill the fathers before they see
      What they have   become.

George Zimmerman

Even the part-time
Labour-adverse
Small-scale beat-cops.

The ones with the badges
Shinin' like polished
Rainfall, blistered like
Pock-marked suburbia.

Even with their
Insipid metaphors
And their short-fuse
For wrong-day
Bin-deliveries.

Be the minotaur
You know the streets
Like song to a prayer
For acid rain.

Guide 'em.
Grind 'em.
Gut 'em.

Even the neighbourhood-
Watchers. Forgive 'em
As they bleed out, forgive
The street-sweeper who
Cleans 'em up, forgive
Yourself for clenchin'
Their ashen-valve until
The beatings stop.

Amber Guyger

The sick note bobbies bleed quicker, viscous
Like shelter is syrupy, like home ownership

Is tricky. Choke the part time patrolmen
With coffee, spot their cuffs with split lips.

Split their lips. Split their lips wide open.
Home is a hell, make hell a haven, nuzzle

Toothpicks in the blue blood toenails, make
'em kick a door. Teach' em to breathe through

A crimson mist, a torniquet tight headlock.
Teach 'em to bathe in the morning and

Walk away from the church. The first sign
Of a killer is a uniform, emblazened, pride-

Heavy. Bravery is a medal made of scalps,
The skill In givin' up, useless furnishings, fevered

Drowning. Coffee sippers slippin' tips to
Killers, working ten foot and half a sandwich

From a tazer terrorist. Leave 'em half hung
And crow-pecked pupils. Abolish politeness.

Vallejo Police

Take a body count, how many sippin' their
Anti-matter, how many wankin' in witness
Rooms, how many phonin' their families

Tappin' their chalky gums. Petrol wont
Give you a score but it counts cops
On both hands and saves room for sheriffs.

Bottle it in rags and riches, divisive rhetoric
Media-heavy love letters to hogs tied houndin'
Us heathens. Abacus the baton-welders, the riot-

Sweaters, the steel-toe-stompers. Spit sickly
Sweet ulcer pus and bite your blisters
'Til the splinters fracture ferris wheel frenzied.

Chisel dicks onto the marble arches, the police
Pillars of society two whistles from a smashed
Melon for the difference between graffiti and

Vanishing acts. They want us docile, on our
Backs, fluffy side up and tickled – docile
Like sneezing is a movement to occupy,

Docile like protest is a kessel all steam
And lost energy. When they burn remember
How their screams evoke pity and ours

Evoke defiance.

David Duckenfield

All the watchmen: from gatekeepers of valhalla
To vanguards whipping batons on iron
Vesitbules. Squeeze 'em dry.

Block out the sun, the scum festered leeches,
Duct tape its sores and blister every
Whiskey red parasitic nose.

They clamberin' for us parchment paper crisp
Warrants for warrens. Like a blanched
Hare they're loosenin' your

Flesh, primin' the sickle, callin' glory to the
Landlords, to the rent due for walkin'
streets laden with every ounce

Of potential. An excuse is how they play a deck
Bone-heavy with Kings, how they whip
Rib kick spur burn nib to paper -

In every ink pad rests the story of a labyrinth
Tree-ring cultivated journey breakin'
It's own fingers in rapture.

It's how they tell it, how they strike the punchline
Like a match to the ladybug's home.
Fly away, fly away,

Your children are gone.

Darren Wilson

First there is the reckoning.
First there is the reckoned with.
Have you ever walked a hall
Like a boatman sailing styx?

Even they holster their oars
In uncertainty. The virus drinks
Joe by the gallon, gloats into
Mirrors, chews over questions

Like that one owl that sleeps
Face down. Reckoned. I'm told
A small needle in an exact
Position on the back of the neck

Is enough to take down a deputy.
You'll want a sting to fall bigger
Game. Grenadine. Grenadine.
We think in differing cocktails.

We delouse ourselves before
We devour. We deign to laws
Set in bone splint shins split
Thin paper thin sprint to break

Spines. The reckoned then
The reckoning. The vultures
Beak burnt from picking carcass,
It still cooks when taken from

The coop, still boils when the
Whip is lighter than the book.
A knife in the gut should come
Out clean if inserted correctly,

Twist for effect. Twist for respect.
The sweetest lesson is counting
Double for every cop that beats
Drum sound check music neck

Split reckon / (ed) with. Council
Kids chew shoes like blue bruise
Like cops cruise for licking,
Kick the stick in. Battin' for baton,

Kneecap them before they
Stomp like a Tory snorting
Snow banging chamber floor
To police percussion, the welfare

State of it all. We've been taught
To listen before we could pluck
The words from the intent and
Interpret violence. A means

To an end, a reckoning, a full
Scale cocktail. Red rags lit
Red. Blue bloods bit blue.

Timothy Loehmann

They sing songs when it rains. They like the sound of windscreen wipers squeegeeing blood. They eat burgers after murders and doughnuts after abuse. They prefer their glass two way and their conversations one way. They think window shopping is the first step to suspicious activity, it is an advert for comeuppance. They touch their coffee with their little finger first, they can still hold a baton without their pinky, some prefer to point their pinky when holding a baton to retain some dignity in the face of bone fractures. They're never caught out at home. They light tealights in the evening to cover up the scent of their afternoon. They will use either nostril but find it easier snorting with the right one. They can still work on coke but they struggle on amphetamines. They know which radiator pipes can bear the weight of a scared teenager. Their favourite plants are succulents, daffodils, and in the glovebox. They count shrapnel to count bullets because counting bullets requires a thought process in media res. They bear arms and bare arms to look for evidence, a track is the first step to the mechanism revealing itself. They like it when the mayor plays along. They admire shoplifters who do it to escape the boredom of financial security. They prefer to look in mirrors face on because they do not like to profile themselves. They take the trash out in pairs for fear of not returning home, they wait until morning and sprint to feel alive, they do not care if the bag splits. They eat until the sides burst and then they eat the streets eat the people filing I the rain to be eaten by the greed and sheer audacity of it all. They are the reason parents look under beds. They console themselves with indigestion. They are humanity, peak humanity, peak inhumane magnamity offering a handshake or a squeeze. They eat their young. They eat our young.

Philip Brailsford

It is how they are reticulated in
Bored commission to break a bone

And snake a broken hip joint
Reason to kill a kid snap his neck

Like the first home the way the door
Never shut fully tell 'em you used

To leave' em unlocked so they can
Leave 'em locked right up to the nine

Ten aces booting shit striped heel
Toe leather on a frame bigger

Than any need to correlate traffic
Stops weather in check to inebriate

Like taxes are just how we pay
To bang ourselves up like the system

Is an excuse to ask the system
To forgive us when the system does

What we pay it to do and I would pay
It good money to show us a single

Dirty cop who can out the wretched
Spot they've started to love and caress

As a new pet to guide them in wet
Dreams of the sweet stain salivating

Over matter like brain like dark like
The thud of a report on the desk

Sign where piggy boy wants a quick
Clause and an alibi tighter than a cop's

Ass filled fist deep with snuff with
Powder with every inch of pilfered

Job satisfaction perk tweaking
Harder than caffeine and a weighted

Club to the wrong kid at the wrong
Time a misery collect a prayer

And call it a day with two bullets
Hotter than a hole burnt through

 pension-heavy bank account

Jeronimo Yanez

It isn't the way you
move through
Grass like blood to
crease
Like crease to pit to
street
To a rendering of
observance
As a means of futile
survival

It isn't the way you
shield
Children like the
nurture
Matters more than
the nature
Matters more than
pistol
Whip bullet fly slip
sheet

It isn't the sides cho-
sen
By colour by instinct
led
By tax haven waiting
For a reason to keep
cool
While BEAT RAW
BEAT RAW

It isn't hope in the
flight
Of birds penning
themselves
In open air guided
chest
Cavity torn hole like
a closed
Window on a sum-
mer's shame

It isn't you it's them
their waste
Their calm eyes
open guise
Wait for trigger fin-
ger line
Orchids in late wait
for
An excuse to pin
blame

Acknowledgements

The Rink was published by *Dostoyevsky Wannabe*

Bampy was published by *Hesterglock Press' Protex(s)t* imprint

Tertiary Colours was published by *Knives, Forks, and Spoons Press*

St Day Road was published by *Broken Sleep Books*

Last Hundred was published by *Guillemot Press*

Blood Fjord '89 was published by *Glyph Press*

SHITSHOW was published by *Legitimate Snack*

Melatonin Spring Collection was published by *Invisible Hand Press*

Harbour Equinox was published by *Sampson Low*

Perfectly Reasonable Justifications for Nuclear Apocalypse was published by *And False Fire*

LAY OUT YOUR UNREST
&
ARREST THE COPS WHO
KILLED BREONNA TAYLOR

Lightning Source UK Ltd.
Milton Keynes UK
UKHW022021090221
378511UK00005B/245

9 781913 642464